MEGA BOOKS

AIRCRAFT

CHRISTIANE GUNZI
AND CHEZ PICTHALL

Gareth Stevens
PUBLISHING

**Please visit our website,
www.garethstevens.com.
For a free color catalog of all
our high-quality books, call
toll free 1-800-542-2595 or
fax 1-877-542-2596.**

Published in 2025 by
Gareth Stevens Publishing
2544 Clinton St.
Buffalo, NY 14224

Designer: Paul Calver
Written and edited by: Christiane Gunzi and Chez Picthall
Editorial assistant: Katy Rayner
Aviation consultant: Keith Wilson

Images: AgustaWestland; Alain Demonty *www.al-airliners.be*; Andrew Gadd/Redhill Airshow; Bombardier Aerospace; Brian Lockett; Cessna Aircraft Company; Chad Thomas www.*jetwashimages.com*; Craig Murray; Diamond Aircraft; E.J.Van Koningsveld *www.sky-flash.com*; Emiel Sloot/STAS Aviation Press; Eric Van Gilder *www.vg-photo.com*; Fred Seggie; Groen Brothers Aviation, Inc.; Harry Follas; Jim Koepnick/EAA; Keith Wilson; Lockheed Martin Aeronautics Company; M. Van Leeuwen *www.zap16.com*; Mark van der Vliet; Max "Foxbat" Bryansky; Mike Evans; Moller International, U.S.A; NASA (Jim Ross; NASA/Harrop; Nick Galante/PMRF; Tom Tschida; Tony Landis); Neil Stuart Lawson *www.whiteplanes.com*; P&M Aviation Ltd; Petr Popelář; Richard Vandervord; Robert Roggeman; Tropical Biplanes *www.tropicalbiplanes.com*; WP Aviation; Zenith Aircraft Company

Cataloging-in-Publication Data

Names: Gunzi, Christiane. | Picthall, Chez.
Title: Aircraft / by Christiane Gunzi and Chez Picthall.
Description: Buffalo, NY : Gareth Stevens Publishing, 2025. | Series: Mega books
Identifiers: ISBN 9781482468366 (pbk.) | ISBN 9781482468373 (library bound) | ISBN 9781482468380 (ebook)
Subjects: LCSH: Airplanes--Juvenile literature. | Airplanes, Military--Juvenile literature.
Classification: LCC TL547.G85 G86 2025 | DDC 629.133'34--dc23

Printed in the United States of America

CPSIA compliance information: Batch #CSGS25: For further information contact Gareth Stevens at 1-800-542-2595.

CONTENTS

Light Aircraft 4

Passenger Planes 6

Transporters 8

Fast Jets 10

Supersonic Aircraft 12

Float Planes 14

Biplanes and Triplanes 16

Classic Planes 18

Helicopters 20

Fire Fighters 22

Stunt Planes 24

Fun Aircraft 26

Space Planes 28

Amazing Planes 30

Glossary & Index 32

LIGHT AIRCRAFT

Small aircraft that are used for sport and for touring are called light aircraft. They usually have space for four people. Some light aircraft are sold as kits. People can build them at home in a garage or workshop.

Vans RV-7A

CGS Aviation Ultra Hawk

Kit plane

This two-seat Vans plane is the most popular kit aircraft. Some kit planes use the same kind of fuel as cars. This one flies at 217 miles (350 km) an hour.

Ultralight

This is a very light kit plane with just one seat for the pilot. It can fly at 85 miles (137 km) an hour. Some ultralights also carry a parachute so that the pilot can land safely if the engine stops.

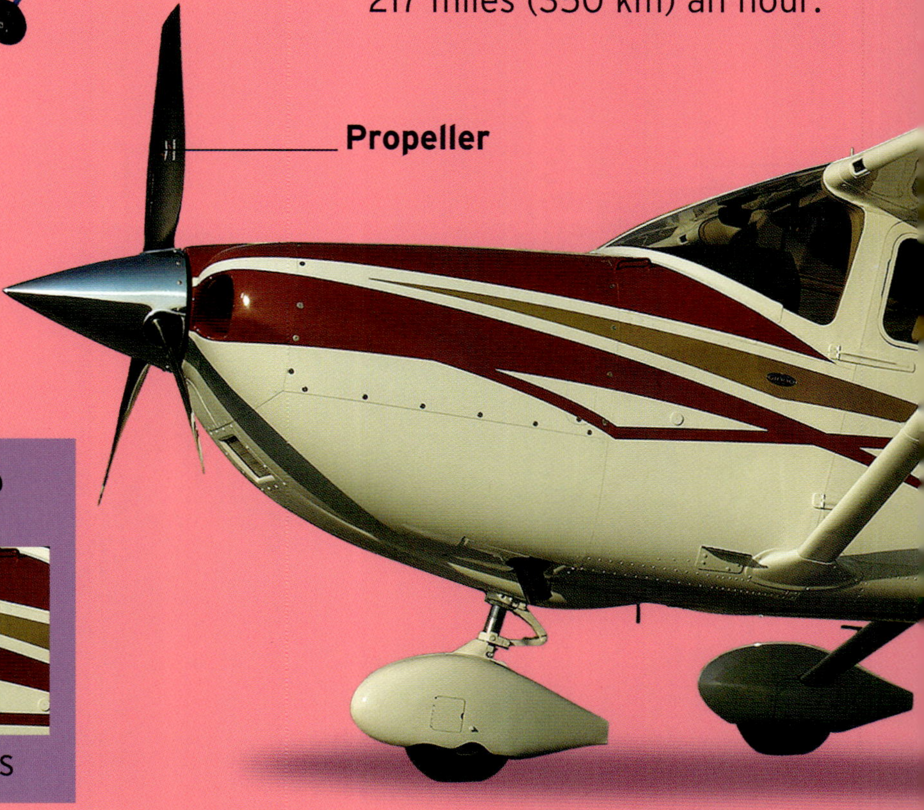

Propeller

Can you point to?

pilot

letters

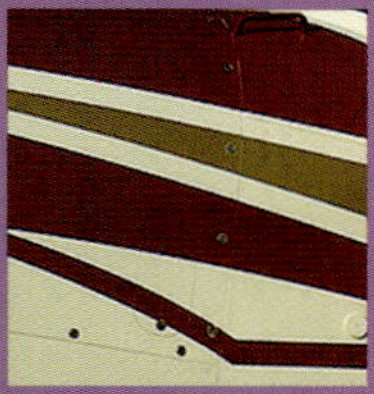

stripes

Diamond Twinstar

This exciting modern aircraft is made of carbon fiber and has diesel engines like the ones in Mercedes cars. Its winglets help it to fly fast. It can fly 223 miles (359 km) an hour!

Where are the winglets?

Cessna Skylane

This is one of the world's most popular single-engine planes. Cessna Skylanes were first built in 1956, and are still made today. They are built of aluminum-alloy and fly at 173 miles (278 lm) an hour.

PASSENGER PLANES

Big airplanes that people take to go on vacations far away are called passenger planes. These aircraft include jumbo jets and airbuses. Passenger planes fly to every country in the world and can carry hundreds of people.

Bombardier

This is one of the fastest long-range jets, and it flies at about 565 miles (909 km) an hour. It has enough seats for 15 passengers and is very comfortable. There is even a bedroom on board!

Boeing 747

A Boeing 747 is nicknamed the "jumbo jet." This aircraft has an upper and lower deck, with two rows of windows. There are seats for up to 525 passengers.

Boeing 747

Which big plane has a bedroom?

Airbus A380

This is the world's biggest passenger aircraft. An Airbus A380 has seats for up to 853 people and can fly for 9,450 miles (15,208 km) without stopping. It costs about $200 million to build just one!

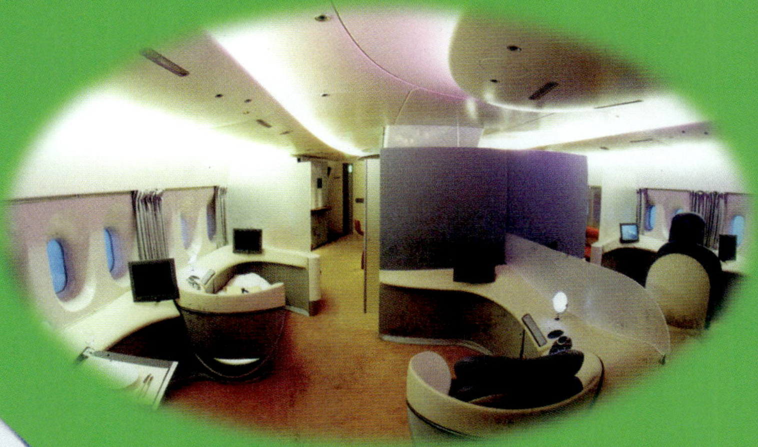

Airbus A380

Luxury on board

Some new planes are well-equipped. They have desks and computers so passengers can work during the flight.

Can you point to?

numbers

windows

leaf

TRANSPORTERS

Mega aircraft called transporters carry all sorts of heavy cargo and equipment around the world. Some transporters are strong enough to carry trucks, trains, and even space rockets! These special aircraft are used to deliver supplies in emergencies.

Can you point to?

stripe

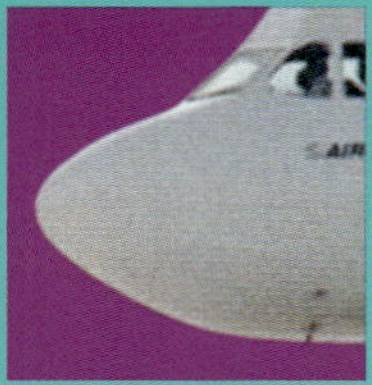
nose

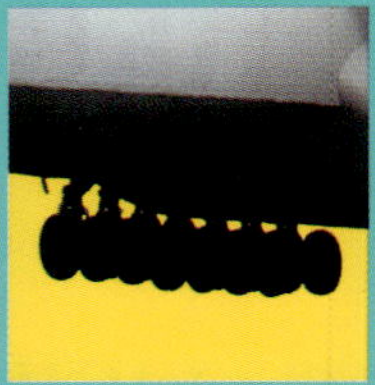
wheels

Which plane is named after a whale?

Antonov An-225 Mriya

Wheels

Mega loads

Big transport aircraft often carry heavy vehicles like trucks from one country to another. The trucks get on to the plane by backing up into the front part.

Airbus A300-600ST Beluga

Beluga

This transporter is known as "Beluga" because it looks like a whale. It transports helicopters and huge machinery, and can carry up to 52 tons (47 mt). The cockpit is low so the cargo door opens upwards.

Antonov An-225 Mriya

This is the world's largest aircraft. It was designed to carry space rockets and trains. An Antonov can also transport supplies and can carry up to 705 tons (640 mt). It has 32 wheels!

Lockheed Martin C-5 Galaxy

This American transporter is one of the world's biggest military aircraft. Its cargo area can carry large vehicles and its upper deck has seats for 73 passengers. The passengers sit facing backwards!

Lockheed Martin C-5 Galaxy

FAST JETS

Some aircraft are so fast that they fly at twice the speed of sound. These planes are called supersonic jets. Fighter jets are used by air forces in many countries. They are quick, agile, and can even fly upside down!

Lockheed Martin F-22A Raptor

Raptor

The top speed of this fighter jet is a secret, but experts agree that it flies at over 1,300 miles (2,092 km) an hour. About 100 of these have been made. Each one costs about $233 million!

Can you point to?

wheel

nose cone

numbers

Which of these jets is red, white, and blue?

Lockheed Martin F-16 Fighting Falcon

Fighting Falcon

These lightweight fighter jets have one seat for the pilot and can fly at 1,520 miles (2,446 km) an hour. Over 4,000 have been built since 1976. They can travel in any kind of weather and can fly straight up!

Typhoon

These jets have two engines and can climb 62,000 feet (18,897 km) a minute. The air forces in Italy, Germany, Spain, and the UK fly them. Typhoon jets cost about $79 million!

Dassault Rafale

SUPERSONIC AIRCRAFT

Supersonic planes make a loud booming sound when they fly past. This is called breaking the sound barrier. Some planes are used for carrying passengers and cargo. A few supersonic aircraft are used for spying!

Can you point to?

logo

light

triangles

Tupolev Tu-144

The Russian Tupolev Tu-144 was the first supersonic transport aircraft. It was also the fastest commercial aircraft built to carry mail and cargo.

Concorde

Only 20 of these were ever built, and they flew from London to New York in 3.5 hours. The Concorde traveled at over 1,330 miles (2,140 km) an hour, twice as fast as other planes. Its "droop-snoot" nose lowered during takeoff and landing to help the pilot to see clearly.

Lockheed Blackbird

This amazing SR-71 Blackbird is used for spying. It is one of the fastest and highest-flying aircraft ever built. From 80,000 feet (24,384 m) up, a pilot could photograph a car's license plate!

Which supersonic plane can fly the highest?

Fastest flier

An SR-71 flew over 2,000 miles (3,219 km) an hour from New York to London in under 1 hour and 55 minutes—a world record!

FLOAT PLANES

Planes that are able to land on water are called float planes. These special flying boats can land on rivers, lakes, or the sea. Some have wheels which they lower to drive on dry land.

Can you point to?

rectangle

circle

triangle

Where can you see some floats?

Consolidated PBY Catalina

Amphibian

This four-seat aircraft has a pair of floats for landing on water. These floats make it higher off the ground than normal so it has some steps too.

Catalina

The American Catalina is one of the most famous flying boats ever built. It was used in World War II. Its big "blister" windows help the team to see clearly all around.

BIPLANES AND TRIPLANES

Old aircraft are slow and noisy, but exciting to fly and fun to watch. A biplane has two sets of wings and a triplane has three. They were used in two world wars, and became popular as crop dusters and sports planes.

Boeing Stearman

These biplanes are popular at air shows. Acrobats do daring displays by standing and walking on the wings.

Pitts S-2C

Antonov AN-2

Antonov biplane

The Russian Antonov is the largest single-engine biplane ever built. Its undercarriage can be replaced with floats or skis instead of wheels. It is used to carry cargo, fight fires, spray crops, and as an ambulance. There are about 5,000 of these around the world.

Fokker triplane

This old German triplane was used in World War I as a fighter plane. It is very well known and now does flying displays at air shows.

Fokker Dr.1 Triplane

Where can you see a picture of a panda?

CLASSIC PLANES

Old planes that are popular and famous are called classic. They are not as fast or powerful as the modern aircraft that we use today, but these planes are rare, so they are very special.

Can you point to?

tail fin

propeller

star

Constellation

In the 1940s and 1950s, this plane flew people from New York to London and Paris, and it was used by all the big airlines. It had four piston engines and its tail had three fins.

Douglas DC-3

The Douglas DC-3 passenger plane first flew in 1935 and was the first U.S. aircraft that had a kitchen on board. It could fly for 1,000 miles (1,609 km) without stopping for fuel.

Mustang

This North American plane is one of World War II's most famous aircraft. It had a top speed of 437 miles (703 km) an hour and could climb 2,300 feet (700 m) a minute. Many aircraft were named by their crew and this one is called "Six-shooter."

Spitfire

This British single-seat aircraft is super famous. It has a Rolls-Royce Merlin engine and a top speed of 408 miles (657 km) an hour.

HELICOPTERS

Helicopters are popular aircraft that often do important jobs. They are used by the police, as air ambulances, and for sea rescues. They are speedy and can take off, fly, and land in places where other aircraft cannot go.

R22 Beta II helicopter

Columbia

This Boeing helicopter is a type of Chinook military aircraft. It has two rotors to lift it off the ground and four sets of wheels for landing. These aircraft are used to rescue people and also to put out forest fires.

Columbia Boeing Vertol 234UT

RAF Sea King

Sea King

This helicopter has two pilots, a radar operator, and a winchman. It rescues people on cliffs, mountains, and at sea. It has room for three stretchers and can lift a person on a winch. Sea Kings help to save many lives.

BAAC BA609

Tiltrotor

This Bell/Agusta Aerospace Company tiltrotor is a mixture of a helicopter and an airplane. Tiltrotor aircraft can fly twice as fast as ordinary helicopters. They are often used for search and rescue at sea. They fly in any weather, including snow and ice.

FIRE FIGHTERS

Some kinds of helicopters and planes fight forest fires. These special aircraft have tanks that carry water or a liquid that puts out fires. Other firefighters called waterbombers pick up water from lakes and rivers.

Can you point to?

number

tail rotor

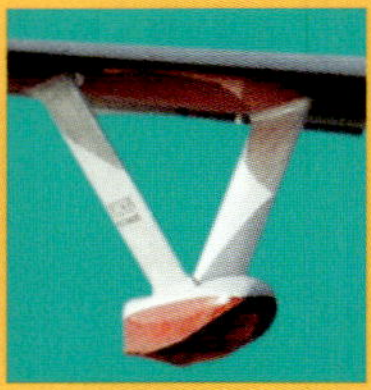

triangle

Martin Mars Waterbomber

Waterbomber

This is the largest flying boat that fights fires. It lands on a lake or river, then scoops up water, which takes only 25 seconds. Two waterbombers working together can drop over 7,130 gallons (27,000 l) of water every seven minutes.

Lockheed P-3A Air tanker

Where is the bendy hose?

Helitanker

This S-64 Aircrane helitanker is a powerful and useful flying firefighter. It can carry 2,640 gallons (10,000 l) of water. Its hose can suck up water from lakes, rivers, or the sea in under 45 seconds.

Aircraft putting out a fire

Air tanker

This aircraft was first used by the U.S. Navy and it has been turned into a waterbomber. Its fleet number is on the nose and tail.

STUNT PLANES

Flying teams that do cool tricks and fly very fast are called aerial display teams. They perform at amazing air shows and entertain people all over the world. Only the most skilled pilots do this job because it is so dangerous.

F-16C Fighting Falcons

Thunderbirds

The Thunderbirds team of the U.S. Air Force fly Fighting Falcon jets at over 1,500 miles (2,414 km) an hour.

British Aerospace Hawks

Red Arrows

The RAF Red Arrows are the world's most famous aerial display team. They use nine Hawk aircraft and have done over 4,000 displays in 53 countries. Hawk aircraft normally fly at 1 mile (1.6 km) every 10 seconds, but they go much slower to perform these aerobatic displays.

Super Corsair

Ten Super Corsairs were built to fight in World War II, but they were never used. Instead, people started to race them. Each plane has a number.

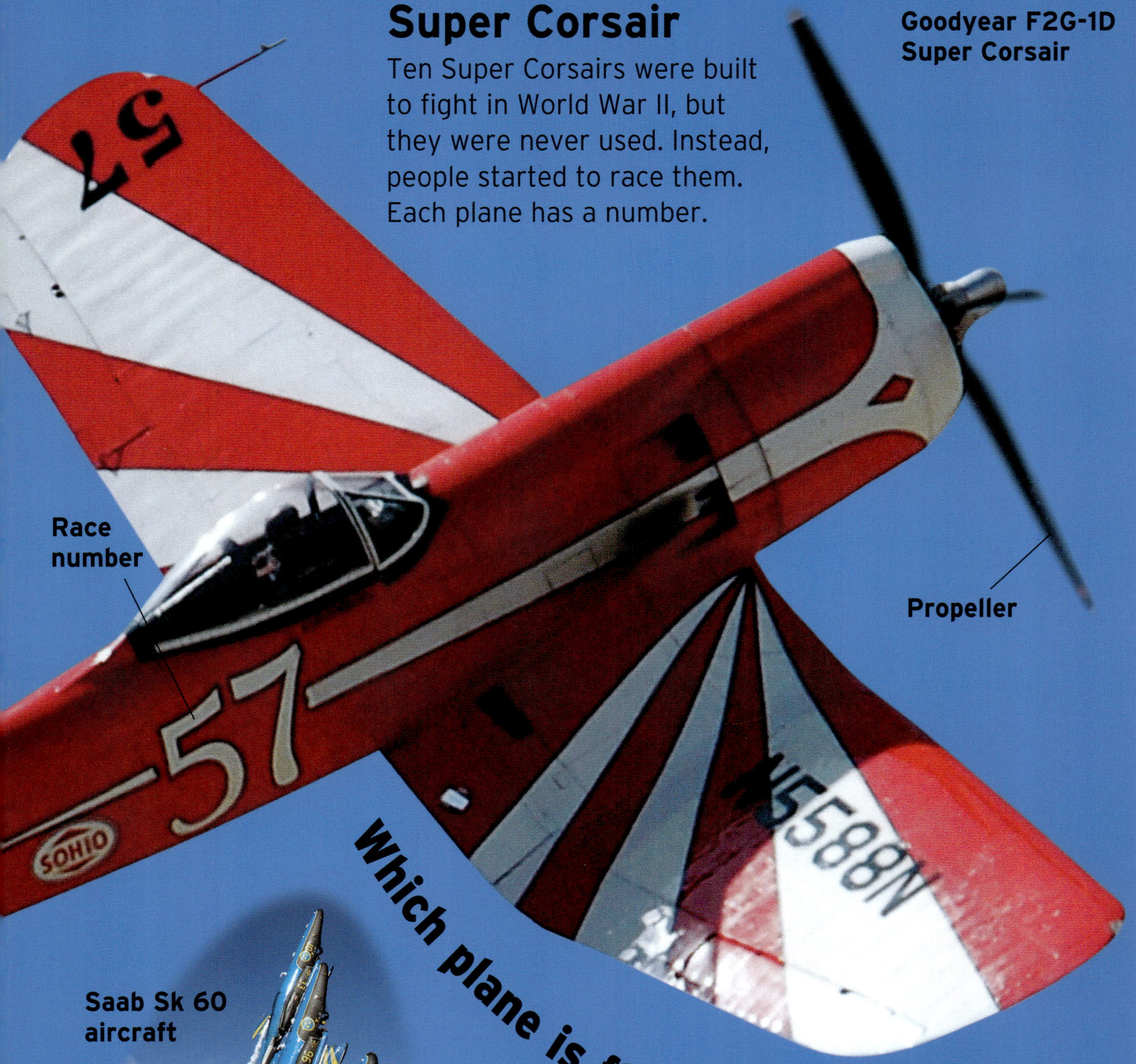

Which plane is flying upside down?

Team 60

The aerobatic team of the Swedish Air Force is called Team 60. They fly colorful Saab Sk 60 high-wing aircraft with twin engines. Most of the pilots who fly these planes are senior flight instructors from the Swedish Air Force.

FUN AIRCRAFT

Some little aircraft are very unusual and fun to fly. There are gliders with no engines, and microlights with no doors or windows. One amazing small plane of the future even looks like a flying car!

NASA Daedalus Project's Light Eagle

Can you point to?

fan

wheel

pilot

Light Eagle

This aircraft was an experiment to see if a person could power a plane. It only weighs 93 pounds (42 kg). In a test flight in 1987, it flew 36 miles (58 km) and set a world record for human-powered flight.

Skycar

This plane of the future is powered by four fans. It takes off like a helictopter and flies at 375 miles (604 km) an hour. There is room for four people. One skycar will cost $630,000!

Moller Skycar

Glider

A glider's wings and body are longer and thinner than a plane's. Most gliders do not have an engine so these aircraft are quiet to fly.

Which unusual aircraft is named after a bird?

Microlight

This microlight looks like a tricycle with a kite on top. It has a top speed of over 100 miles (161 km) an hour, and only uses 3 to 4 gallons (11 to 14 l) of fuel an hour.

SPACE PLANES

A few special aircraft can fly into space and return back to Earth. The space shuttle carries astronauts and cargo to the International Space Station. Planes of the future may be able to travel to new planets!

NASA X-37

NASA X-37

This space plane of the future will be able to travel at 25 times the speed of sound. It may be used to transport crew to and from the space station.

What is the jumbo jet carrying?

Can you point to?

letters

windows

logo

NASA X-43C

This space plane of the future will fly so fast that it will be hypersonic! Its engine will suck in oxygen and mix it with jet fuel to make it travel at over 62 miles (100 km) a minute!

NASA X-43 C

Piggyback ride

A special Boeing 747 jumbo jet carries the space shuttle from the landing site back to the launch site in Florida.

Space Shuttle

The American space shuttle *Atlantis* has spent 220 days in space and has completed 3,468 orbits around Earth. In total, the shuttle has flown 89.9 million nautical miles (166 million km).

Boeing 747 carrying the space shuttle

AMAZING PLANES

Exciting new planes are being made all the time. These test planes of the future are called prototypes. Some are able to fly without a pilot, and others fly using energy from the sun.

Grumman X-29

This strange aircraft looks as if it is flying backwards. It was built by NASA in the 1980s as an experiment.

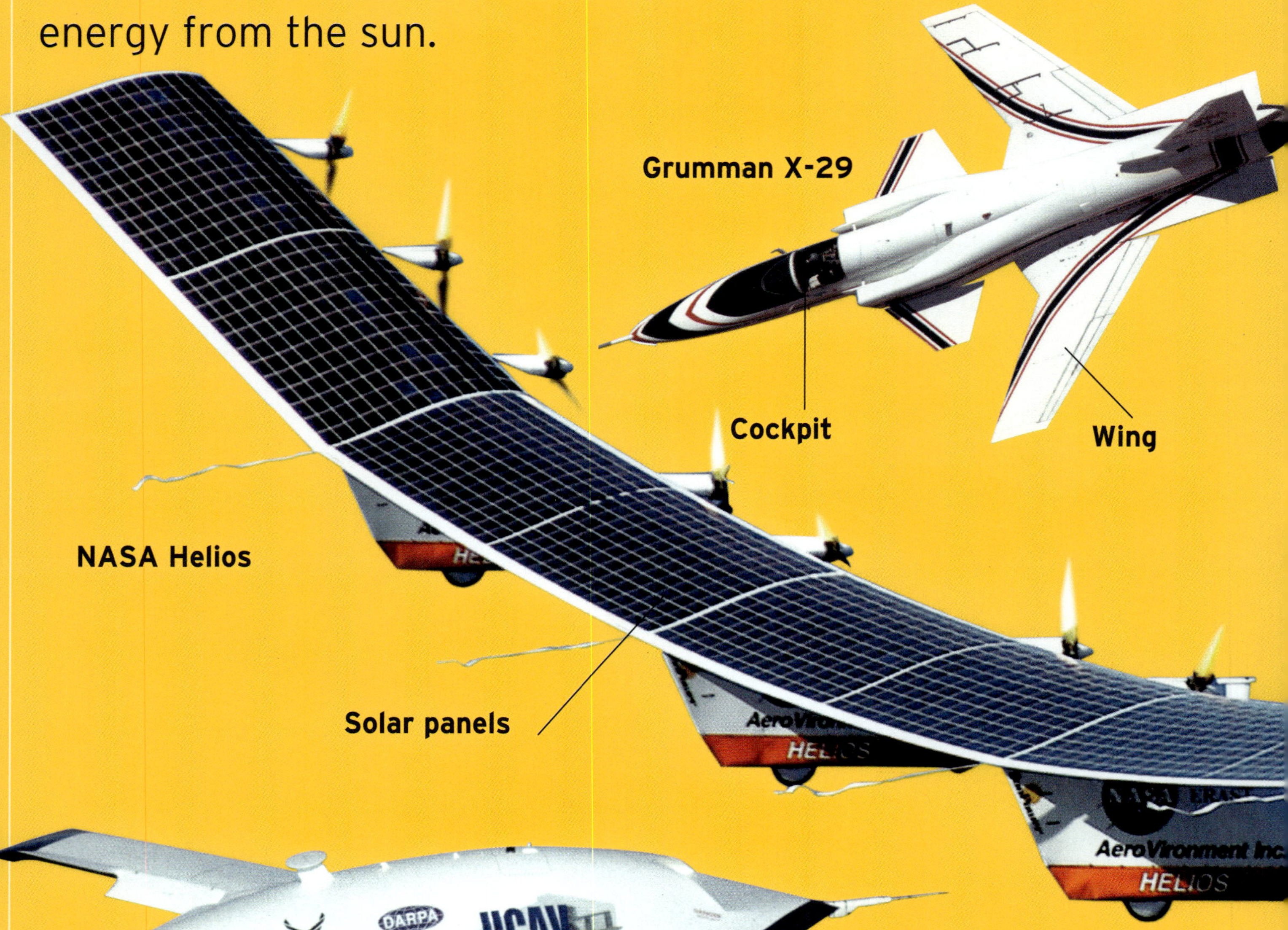

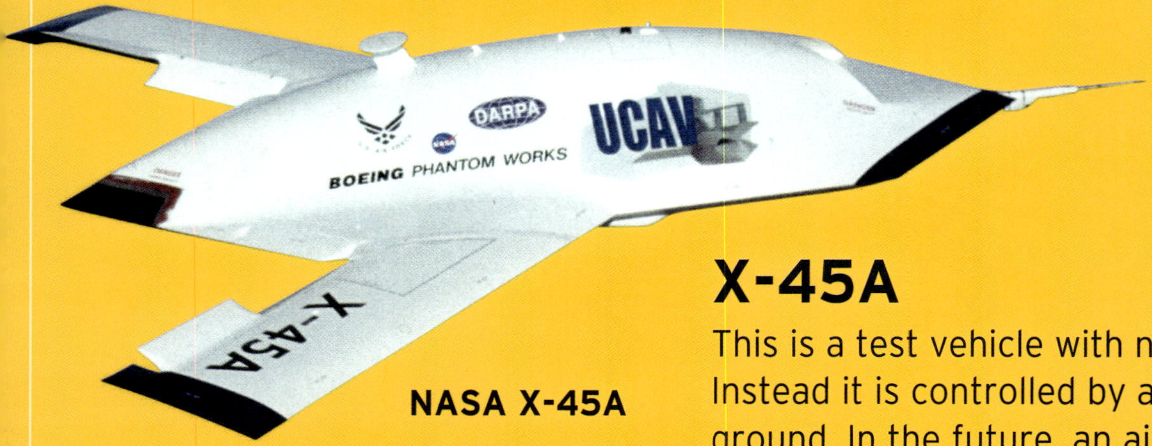

X-45A

This is a test vehicle with no crew on board. Instead it is controlled by a pilot on the ground. In the future, an aircraft like this may be used by the U.S. Air Force and Navy.

Voyager

This was the first aircraft to fly around the world without stopping. The flight took nine days in December 1986, and Voyager flew 26,366 miles (42,432 km). This aircraft is in the Smithsonian Museum in Washington, DC.

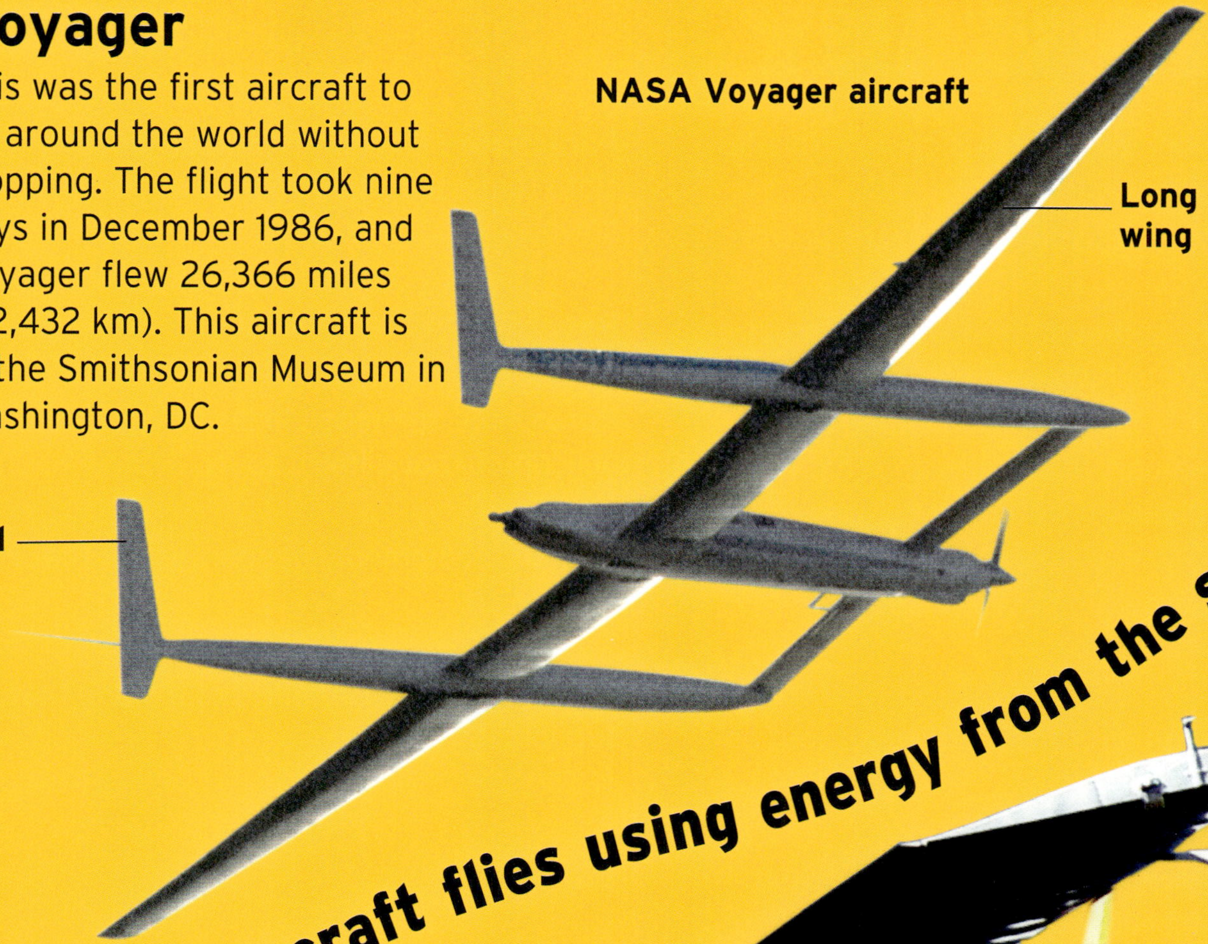

Which aircraft flies using energy from the sun?

Helios

Helios was a lightweight flying wing built by NASA. Its solar panels were powered by energy from the sun. Helios could fly for weeks or months at a time. It flew to 96,864 feet (29,524 m) high!

Can you point to?

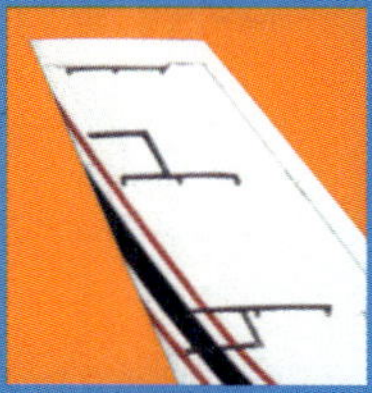

wing

solar panels

letters

GLOSSARY

Deck - one of the levels on an airplane.

Engine - a machine that makes power.

Expert - someone who knows a great deal about something.

Float - a part of the airplane that holds up the airplane on water.

Fuel - something used to make energy, heat, or power.

Glider - an aircraft that flies without an engine.

Hypersonic - having to do with being five times the speed of sound.

Parachute - a specially shaped piece of cloth that collects air to slow something down.

Rare -uncommon or special.

Rotor - the spinning blades on top of a helicopter that allow it to fly.

Stunt - a commonly dangerous act that is hard to do.

Undercarriage - the parts of a plane that support it.

INDEX

aerial display teams 24
Airbus 6, 7, 9
air force 10,11, 24, 25, 30
American Catalina 15
Boeing 747 7, 29
cargo 8, 9, 12, 16
Cessna Skylane 5
Concorde 12
Douglas DC-3 18, 19
fighter jets 10
forest fires 20, 22
Fokker triplane 17
glider 26, 27
Helitanker 23
jumbo jet 6, 7, 28
kit plane 4
Lockheed SR-71 Blackbird 13
P-51 Mustang 19
Red Arrows 24
rescue 20, 21
space shuttle 28, 29
Spitfire 19
supersonic jets 10, 12, 13
Team 60 25
Thunderbirds 24
Tiltrotor 21
world record 13, 16
World War I 17
World War II 15, 19, 25